The Disappearing Cowboy Trick

The Disappearing Cowboy Trick

Kristin Abraham

Horse Less Press
2013

ISBN: 978-0-9829896-4-7

Cover art collage by HR Hegnauer
Images from the Library of Congress:
    "Jones Barn where dynamite was found"
        George Grantham Bain Collection
    "Sir Genille Cave Brown Cave"
        George Grantham Bain Collection
    "Collision between two engines, Bay of Quinte Railway, ON, 1892"
        Notman photographic Archives - McCord Museum
    "Rustico Beach, PE, 1916 (?)"
        Notman photographic Archives - McCord Museum
Design & typesetting by HR Hegnauer | hrhegnauer.com
Typeset in Goudy Old Style

The publication of this book was made possible through the generous
contributions of our readers and supporters.

HORSE LESS PRESS
www.horselesspress.com

for Matt

always—

Our Hero Writes Home

And then, leaving, we paused before his new machine. "A stress wrangler," he said, upon our asking. "For people who hear God ticking faster and faster." *What does that sound like?* "You'll know it when you need it—everything is a warning sign for something else." He proceeded to wind the crank. The gears zipped and whistled, levers pumped like elbows. The air was full of grease. Surely we knew this was some other kind of ruse to put up next to the mermaid girl, the cooch dancers, the tank with the turtle boy. Yet mesmerizing—gorgeous and curling over on itself. *Hell's fire and little fishes*, we whispered. "You see, noticing is the beginning of wisdom." All we could do was nod and thicken up. There's no getting around a wink and a warning.

ONE

Little Miss Skeleton in Her Closet

Years later, in the town's only lake, the lantern's ray
sifts the green water and flickers at its own farthest
yellow arm, cloudy with silt trailing into
and out of this light—as if saying *follow me, here*
is where you'll find it, coaxing toward pitch
and muck: the rusted-out car gone over
the bridge, with its bride and the hole in her
head, veil trailing, fish-nibbled, into the gloam;
golf balls shot from the banks, arrows zinged
in carp season; old burlap packed with litters
of puppy bones; wagon wheels; antlers; rust-crusted
coffee pots. It was supposed to be content,
how we had always thought of this water, surveyed
across the still surface, so close to cracking, sick
of playing pretend all the time in our heads.

Things that are muffled, open—

We start off slow like this, red. Watch
the stones tipping off our shoes, the snow.
Each second small and aspirin flavored,
the learning of childhood. *May I sit? May I
stand?* Look both ways, please & thank you.
(Curtsy to the crowd.) (Pause for applause.)
May I sit? The world is gathering itself up
to answer, making hesitant checkmarks.
May I stand? Lists of hurt already long
enough. *Long enough*, the world begins,
begins a sigh. We're looking at the cracks
in the lampshade. Looking for the yellow
to come through: the biology, electricity,
like math; meaning, the more we touch it,
the more it spreads. Like menthol, heat
rash. The louder it gets. *Stand back—
I'm going to need that air.*

Insidious Dream Waltz

The fifth time he tested his limit, the limit snapped out like a rope and swung a loop back at him. The fifth time, she watched with a heart of crumbling salt, turned dull eyes to the ground when he glanced over. The fifth time and she knew he was cursed—cursed and they too late to move; too tossed off in a dusty, rocky world for her to run to Mother's back porch morning glories; too tossed off, even, to run to a predictable path: wagon trains and sideshow circuits. So when the sky burst into cutlery, rained sterling spoons and butter knives, she was sure it was a fever dream. She was sure she was dying when he plucked a fork from his forearm, considered its shine, wondered why there was no color in that place, except the sky. Wondered why even the sky rejected him so thoroughly. But his words came out so wrong: *We can sell this*, he said. *We'll sell it and run.*

Little Red Riding Hood, Lips like Vinyl

She knew aspirin institutions,
their relevant sounds, was nervous
and bitter from birth with
no evident cause. She had a secret
gash in her palm from holding on
to the edges of everything too long:
countertops, rims of bowls,
book bindings, frames. As accident
would have it, she let go for a while,
her guard down the way children's
guards go down in fairytales. She got
lost and torn in the forest, must have
run toward the hunter in flame orange
gear, realizing too late that he was gunning
her down. He listened to the rifle snap
and ratchet, then saw the residual haunt
of her, caustic like her body, tossing back
and forth, grasping at twigs and snapping
in her pointy boots and pearl buttons.

A Study of *If*

Inevitably, it seemed, the atlas disappeared. That is, lines of demarcation, topographical keys, ridges and water, did not merely bleed together, they bled away. In their place: four black hats in a line on the surface of what one could only presume had been a desert. Hard-packed yellow. Dust-dry. The size of a typical drink coaster. It had become its own small part of the coffee table, flush with the wood on all sides. Self-contained. During cocktail parties, etc., the guests amused themselves by making finger puppets with the hats, and putting their faces to the table to feel the warmth from the sands. They pressed fingers into piles of miniscule rocks, which may or may not have been even smaller hats (there was much debate). Guests prayed to see a lizard, a dust storm, some sign of life, but the longer it was there, the more they believed this was no earthly plot of land. For the first time, they questioned why it was, and how it got there. Some believed it was heaven; some believed hell; others began to wonder *If places could have ghosts, would this be one?* And *Which place is this, haunting us?* The owner, who was not a betting man, began to take bets. He dealt, he said, in *currencies of salvation*, and with each forefinger, plugged his ears theatrically. *I can hear it,* he said: ocean-sound. *This is heaven,* he said, *pays in shells or hats, whichever you prefer.* The others heard it as bug-hum: *Hell,* they said, *heat and locusts in the trees.* It turned into a standoff (the lack of the fear of God versus the one fearing for them all): little boys in front of mirrors, pulling wooden guns at themselves, cocking their hats and clicking their tongues, their impossible teeth.

Call Our Hands *the animals*

Something had burst.
The birds weren't singing.
The children (*we have nothing to do*)
had gathered them:

Lined them up
one by one,
tapping their
walnut heads

Until someone said
What does a gizzard look like?
Where is the wishbone?

They tackled it like that:
wing by wing until
their Band-Aids ripped loose—
little post cards of gauze—

And the hush at their feet
aimed itself upward,
like needles, troubled
pieces of silver.

The Choice between Someone & Somebody

It took him 30 years to vanish into thin air, that place under the beef of his breath. First, the God-fearing eyes, thumb like a bolt. Then, his scars, a cow-skull pelvis, the bone-space between his legs. The ads the town placed just a few years back were for a proper rogue: "Ours is torn and faded." "Like harp strings, the thin spots in cloth." "The wind here is full of wind, and he's becoming like air, not air, air." They were right: each day more like a corn-husk mattress rustle, the space of a tumbleweed. Then that part of him that was wizened, mule-faced, went like the Rapture—holy sweat-and-shake. Went with a small warm spot in his stead.

Good for Our Hero, Good for His Love

Never had such chasing and charging cowered a man so much. But he bit the bullet, watched the blotchy dog kicking up through the sage, heard the sound of his own boots on the boards moments before he fell like a beef. All of this, memory, like so much breeze blowing around his head, so much spit and dust clinging to his cheek, so much of his chest, so much of his ear, pressed to the earth: the sound of the empty laundry tub warping in the heat; the booming store at the back of his throat; and his eyes winging on the door. *No one ever told her no.*

Hair of the Dog

When he realized he could cause dreams,
he started with his horse. *Run*, he said,
and the horse stomped and pawed in its
sleep. *Fly*, he said, and it twitched and
shook.

This must be how God discovered himself.
Then, *Cry*, he commanded his sleeping
wife. She spilled out of the joints in her
lids. *Drown*. She coughed, sputtered, head
from side to side.

How power can stop accumulating, he
could not be sure. All he could do was
gather his breath, assume his role, *do what
I'm meant to do*. So he clapped his hands
and flakes of stone and clay turned to rain
from his palms.

He made them dream death and penance,
made them tie it around their wrists like
balloons. *I'll teach them consequences.* Then
his life was nothing but checking to make
sure everyone was breathing.

And the story began, though he was
mysteriously absent when it ended, hat in
hand, standing on the mountain, looking
down as if in shame at what he had done,
at his wife and horse in the dirt.

Little Red Riding Hood as a Rubber Ducky

She came from a world where neglect was bad:

isolation and the wrong kind of color in her face;

now she's floating down the river to Grandma's

    (*Like Moses. Like Noah.*

    And when I grow up, I'm gonna love).

With two baskets. Two stiff, heavy wings.

Her yellow rain jacket snapped tight—

    puncture and *hiss*,

    running in her head,

    two reds on the inside.

Milk-Ghost Man

He was not drowning;
he was mimic and fury,
which, like fate, began
with a thrash, then was
on him like *normal.*
His death left him stunned,
as if popped in the chops:
the hue and cry, bruise
to his eyes. He had
known that slate blue,
body blue (veins under
the tongue, drained muscles),
but not the calling in his head,
like calling to cattle, fast
like Spanish. Not the words
closing behind him like water—
too much body—arms
folding back into position.

Fits, Starts, Etc.

(It wasn't as simple as

"wife kills husband with hatchet.")
Beginning, in Ohio, where
the farmland takes place
(*great shot; now let's find your*
bird). Ending as a child,
whispering *I don't know*
where this has been. Certain
things we've done since:
sugar on the strawberries,
lemon juice on apple slices.
Inside somewhere, still, that
I'll glow when I want to.
(tendency to burn, etc.)
I tried to not, but couldn't.

TWO

Up to and Including

the time of the fire, which does not include the time of her death. But—some would say—that fire was ultimately the cause of her strife, or much strife, which did lead directly to her demise, although—most would agree—did not actually cause her death. Instead—or because of, or in spite of—she had said, just after the last spark (and the sparks lasted for years), she was often where she started: *a drought summer, leaves and grass with the sound of breathing, the swallowness of the nights.* She said that start—or beginning, or jumpiness—was her fast heart—which excludes *soft ticker* or *I'm feeling a little bit dainty.* And her fast heart chased after a horseshoe mustache—though not the mustache of *Watson's Miracle Elixir,* she insists—chased after a cottonade suit, after a rim-fire cigar, *fast and full of fever days.* That particular quote in the paper led us to believe that she learned which parts of the world smelled like wet dog—or worms—which parts of the world smelled like hot wheat, which parts of the world smelled like *him*—and we'll all agree that last was the problem in the end—excluding, of course, *sober and sorry for it.* Something out there, she insisted, smelled like thinking all the time (*momentum is very real*): *just*—or absolutely, or inevitably—*flat flashes of light off the flat riverbed, a slow-moving storm that hovered over our town for hours, days, and never.*

Story

Right now, the question is what you didn't see. The apple. We began with the mother. And the pea. Fruit turning brown, sour with bites. Add an S. Peas were good. Almost too good. And there were mutton chops—So, pick up here. Where the peas left off. She grew them to replace *father*. To keep warm. Add an S. Tossed at the face the hair swarmed. Mama molted. Like dark red meat: the white of the fat, the dense bone sponge. He got the girl where she got too close. He was loose body ran to lost clause. *That* got her, too. Mechanical flies swarmed on her egg. To see if she would notice. Grew *father* to see the letters sprawl. To make her fat. Hard boiled, the way he rides. The ways he tastes S. So it begins the way it peels. So it begins seeds.

Poem as Frontier

Then all of the *she*'s became *he*'s.

We still had buttons up the back,

tin cups and little rigs, but thick

bristling hides, shotguns

in our skirts, startled birds

killing upwards.

The Hero Lyric

He was supposed to tell
someone about his heartache:
a soul possessed by bees,
perfectly crotched,
a stiff-all-over gait—
but that was a long time ago.
He had already looked at
the eclipse & went blind:
went "the business-end
of a bad mistake." So he died
until he could no longer
ignore the sound of pebbles
skittering around him;
he died until he could
no longer feel the loss
of body. Then
he died a little less.

A Stranger Rides into Town

The day when everything stopped meaning was just as abrupt as any other day, but shot through with hopes that it would be the end. Instead, mottled & blue-black Time perched a little longer, and Worry kicked its feet—one, then the other—in the sand. The girls finally slept, stopped turning their hair in their hands; the boys stopped looking at the sky. We stared at each other dumbly, toe-stubbingly quiet, then let our eyes wander to nowhere, water, and back. We looked at the smudges our hands left on white doors, let go our rabbity heartbeats. Because men ride into town all the time. But sometimes a whimper can sound like a bang.

Cash on the Barrel

He uses a ten-inch steel as throwing practice in front of the tent before the show—it's all part of drawing in the rubes, giving them some kind of flash-and-blade memory with their ticket stubs. The show knives are smaller—$3.70 a dozen in the Montgomery Ward catalogue—but real.

She is his target—or its opposite—spinning on a body-sized circle of wood; he throws around her. She plants her feet on the pegs and grabs hold of the thick metal handles. He spins the wheel and everything turns into a bright round star; her skirt flattens to a triangle; her body stretches to a stiff plank. He can't remember the last ticket he bought himself; she can't remember her name anymore, her wandering fraud.

She runs back to when she was a girl—just before him—skirts damp in the morning grass, Mother's bread hands and all those things she is no longer. A different kind of motion.

When the crowd claps, they clap for her bravery, not his skill; for what they imagine is sweat, not her blood, marked on the edges of their tickets—a nickel's worth. They clap for her curtsey that betrays no dizziness, her wisps of hair. Not her prairie-flushed skin, her dull-shine eyes. She is their fear and their wish to spin.

All she has right now is that moment—just before him—when she rode away, seven years old, swinging her fist and lasso at a dreamed-up life, her mother a high-backed invalid chair wheeling to the door and hushing her straight inside: "This is not what we do in town." Gloves, gloves, gloves.

When her hands pull from the pegs and her feet drop, the dogs rush to see her map, her past, to sniff at her wet-iron fingertips; she is strange to them all evening, so far gone.

He told her this much when he found her—it's not about trust or love; it's about position. They depend on their separateness. He trains to throw around a particular space that she may or may not occupy, and she knows she is never really there.

A Volume for the Hero:
How to Search the Soul and What He Might Find

He believes in *come home to roost*; he believes in a wife, a torn handkerchief, a spot of blood from his sliced finger that frost-morning the knife slipped his wooden grip. He believes in the figure, carved from a fallen branch, a toy for small hands to dance on windowsills; he believes in a life with windowsills, a life with windows, a life with a hole in the middle—and beyond: a humble well, a humble yard, two humble hens pulling grubs from the dust. He believes he saw—that once—a June bug walking out the corner of her eye, believes she's been hiding more—yes—a partial wife tucked in the flour bin. It's necessary—he knows—for her to hide self and other threads, metal flecks, mouse pelts and bones; she's a crow, he believes, one fascinated, one frantic. And, he believes, his life is nothing more than what he hears, what words he thinks he must have said, what he fears—and she is the length of a wheel spoke, nothing more than the thumping tympani, bottom of his belated heart.

Little Red Riding Hood, Inside out

Something flared *pain* in her head.

It made sense like we all make sense.

It was a fur coat, smooth legs, a set of teeth—

      something like

            lipstick

      something like

            braille

Snare drums behind the eyes.

Bigger than a Bread Box

A man who thinks
about awe, stops to
think, just a moment,
in the canyon; armadillos
scuttle by like bald little
men, everywhere on their
toes. But he's not thinking
about them, their shyness;
he's looking for the negative
spaces, needing a little more.

Bog

I.

As for the snow,
it only seemed to matter
when it was there,
running interference
patterns between
psychic and *vision*.

2.

Collar / Collarbone.

3.

Inside the scrap of moss,
the woman looked like a
heart, a scar. Inside the
scrap of moss, the body
stayed preserved.

4.

Sight and interference patterns.
Then: *argument, jawbone,*
Then: a bliss-shaped afterward.

5.

Some of the long bones
had evidence of battle wounds,
and her ghost was shrinking.

6.

A little piece of thick
in her mouth.

7.

Her ghost was shrinking.
I should have bitten him
with vigor, should have
felt the bad kind of anger,
like Christ's palms,
up /down.

8.

Evidence she might have bled,
like all of us bleed in our
own houses. But the sight
showed something different:
it was *fear-birds* and *running.*

9.

As for the snow, bleary.
You know the feeling:
ghost wrapped in oilcloth,
landslide in your mouth.

Don't Give up Five Minutes before the Miracle

Shouldn't the frantic roll bits of God
in their mouths. Shouldn't they flush all that
gravel out. Shouldn't it fly. Shouldn't it
scatter. Shouldn't it all. Shouldn't our hero
be redeemed by it all. Smell the dirt in it all.
Rise with it all. But shouldn't our hero, lurid
with feathers, stay like his spurs, stay
like his horse, stay like his standoff
at noon, fight-to-the-death, "I'll skate on you
when hell freezes over," his scorched-out
smell, residual powder.

& Other Similar Stories

The question is why they would gift this book for her birthday. Her third. So impressionable. The cover was soft and her fingerprints were forever after. Her mother's peas in a jar. Tough like a horsefly, dried from the garden. Or mashed like spring, late fall like a housefly. It's not a fruit. Just like she's not her mother's green. Not anymore. Said *anymore* aloud as she wrote it. Slowly around the soft spring. Swamp mush. Read *anticipation* as an open mailbox. Read *red* as White White. He's her orange rind, dancing with glass. Having eaten warm from her mouth, her breath like cinders. When the sleep broke, there was gourd slime. He's her croaking ripe, trophy wife; she is tough stalk on a mattress. They planted her peas. That's when the stories came. Came to vine. She, staring at the apple. Waiting for it to bite.

Little Red Riding Hood Missed the Bus

Somewhere they won't know
she got herself lost.
But she's folding paper sparrows
inside her head; she's trying confession:
Things moving. The corner of my eye.

The camera is above her;
the angle looks down on her small
rosy twirling. But sometimes
the camera is in her eyes. We see the
everywhere she looks—

                    face—

Now she can't even see the trees
for all the forests. Somewhere a log cabin,
a woodstove. The first fantasy was a mistake.
The second had a rag stuffed in its mouth.

At the Hour of His Strange Dying

Frequent goes on where he left her. *Home,* an insignificant display of fluttering hand to throat, patchwork feebleness. An ox paws her eardrum, bile like wax in her mouth; she scatters feed—*chick-chick*—feed, cranks necks and strips feathers. *This is not what our people do.*

Tonight, she folds boredom, his letters into bowties: *Bringing your sugar and print cotton*—twisted, fanned and crimped. The letters don't tell her his lungs are full up with woolies; no love, no bones about it. They don't tell her he won't have any pearls, though she excuses this: *He is not one to rag proper.*

Now, nigh to a hush, he's gone bright pinch around the eyes, rolling up in himself like a bug. His guts are stuffed—cotton and cheat grass—a series of sipped and fibrous breaths; the horses stand over him and steam.

Now, she holds a needle to lamplight and eyes it, sighs out shiny figures like bubbles: drifting strand of o's, shy white corsets, dancing horse, leather lariats and gloves. They bump at the ceiling—*to be owned and fed; my chickens, my ghost outbursts.*

From the sky-pitched distance, he sees her lamp-slippery wrists and *luck* like a bruise she investigates ritually: *My proof.* He hears her turbulence—a tinder of birds—her *I can smell the snow coming.*

In Which His Pilgrims Suffer a Feast of Reason

Dear Prophet—
you have canary lungs,
sensitivities no one
can bear to witness,
sallow pockets under
your eyes, your knuckles
grind like gizzards.

Dear series of concentric
circles—you are plagued
by the voice of an oyster
shell—we no longer see,
we die, we follow
your wagon—your God
is not you; we hitch and listen.

Dear apology—you are a series
of souls; you know pretty
words, curiosities. Fear is
the root of prophecy,
you say, but the root
of infinity, too, we know.

Dear in the world
but not of the world—
you have never been such
kissed-off light; burned
or not burned we will never
know when to unlock. No one
has a psalter for tongues or notions.

Dear thumbprint—
Dear egregious tree—
How does *truculent*
come into the world? Tucks
in its body as a bird
does just before flight—

Jornada del Muerto

January is his direction, like
north or Mississippi, an arrow
both up and down. All points
he can sketch in the dirt: a first,
and a first, and a first.

It's a windy thirty: flakes scratch
his face; the cows barely ribs,
hands of snow belt their hides.
It's dark on this mountain this
night before never.

He is eye-rubbing tired but
set to build Zion. Stubborn
off brilliance, he has a vision:
creosote bushes, raised arms
and rapture.

Ice is a bear, his boots speak
like anger. Then all the world's
insects lay hands, in an instant.
And heat is one room: he hugs
all he knows, like trying to block
the sun with a finger.

THREE

Hunt

To get out

of his constant slice

this house needs windows

      arrow—

arrow—

Meanwhile, Back at the Ranch

I.
(For a second, everything
in his life aligned perfectly,
like solstice.)

2.
(His pitched heart,
its slanted beat,
his frenzy, over worn.)

3.
(All he wanted was
for rain to break him
open, like a stone,
and he: slats between slats:
the rain, scored through.)

4.
(The other him pulled
a hero face, spit into
nothing jars, blinked
marcasite-colored eyes,
made indecency
and choked on it.)

5.

(He rode *because*
like he loved the dry scallop
of her lace.
Her edge.
Her spur, spur.)

6.

(Rode *because* like he
understood the water,
could imitate it like he could
imitate the rain he knew
would never come.)

Mis-Sized Idea

Called him borrowed.
Called him a caution,
called him not worn out
but worn through, never
called the sun; he never called it.
Nightmares taste like coffee
grounds, used hay; he wakes
with the crusts of them around
his eyes: white, the wars
of his life—that one
has thorns—and he's kissing
the hem of her dress, on his knees
in the dirt, kissing the dust
in the air where her dress just
was—now moth-eaten, now
the comments of his heart.

Nasty Things, Those Hearts

– for Matt

In the first room, he fishes for the moon in the water. He writes a roundup: his words bringing the old-boy dog to heel, his words like choking in her storm, like an abandoned lantern, a white hundred. He writes. He forgives.

In the second room, she is seizing. He holds his hands to her head, presses her skull and its scratching frenetic bird; he tethers her with tent hooks and trumpet vine.

In the third room, she tears from her skin those hooks, lets loose his pulleys. Her wreck is personal, some such nowhere.

This is the room that holds her other room. Her room of piled purchases, phrenological maps, papers, papers, purloined pills, a folded argument, a folded love. This room hides her greatest fear. In this room, the worst smile is repetition.

In the fourth room, his fingers lock together, look like brains. He is taller than Jesus in hat and boots, worn and flannel. He persists. The fourth room hides his greatest fear. In this room he dreams up trees and windfalls, hollers *boom* in his sleep. This room is endless, windowless. Is jugular air.

In the fifth room, his lungs are lost in saguaro. He is miles and miles and wire topography. In the fifth room, he works harder, ribs along, listens for *shhhh* with his bad ear.

Wind Her up, Watch Her Go

She put her hands
edge-to-face:

fused fingers,
plastic smell.

> *Would like to have lived*
> *in a hole*
> *in a cinder block,*
> *matted with straw.*

When she came in,
you smelled the cold on her.

You wanted to shake it out of her—

> *The pain*
> *could be worse;*
> *we live*
> *for desire—*

You shake her
till her eyes
flap, that little
plastic ball inside
rattles around.

She wants you
to pull
her hair.

Wish I were
stuck on a thorn,
a thread in the wind.

She is a rubber doll and
you're pushing
your hand in:
she is a toy wheezing
love me.

Wanted
to die, but didn't
know how.

She was
a pear-shaped
sound.

Our Hero Makes an Impression

Noon again, with her "touch-this-and-I'll-burn-it-down" attitude.
Noon, when she stirred coals and sparked after a morning without
words. Noon, when he watched her with the supper dough
through the window; he watched her with the dough, watched it
quiver from her hands like a triumph filled with suns. Then noon,
and the bread was gone, days old, dry, eaten; noon, and more dull
biscuits in the Dutch oven; noon, and he squared his shoulders.
Noon, when he came home and ate cold meats for dinner, when he
wouldn't shuffle his gaze near her face. Noon, he's whiskey-licked;
noon, with a blueberry buckle; noon, she's a wing in a box. Noon,
when they live and they live and they live because they don't know
how to not.

Story

She speaks into her hands,

brightens, pinks;

her lips touch and feint.

For the time being

was a glove, at least

shaped like a glove,

(in which case what else—

It's not that she moves strangely

but it's the ways she makes

her movements strange:

points to the blue constant

vein in her wrist as she leans:

skin like taut cotton, stretches.

The sound is a patch of grass

(I want to be small—

(I want to live inside of it—

but the vein is a soft

tract, a slight blue,

and she begins there,

at the edge.

Never Borrow Trouble

It was a throat-clearer, for sure: the way he walked into town wild, wooly and full of fleas; he was no good for that girl, but we dallied our tongues. Some willful wrong is what it was, some lie. But there they were: a knife-slinging event, a sideshow. They were nomad, carnie, never put down heels—next best thing to rustling beef when a woman can't ride the trail. Then her face got broad, her skirts more full. Circus would go on without them, as circuses tend to do. He'd build a small cabin at the bend in the dry creek; she would sweep. He'd deal faro; she would keep house or sling biscuits at the inn. One day she would die and next day be buried in creosote. Their children would grow to inherit the town. They would have rabbit heartbeats. They would say *It is more dark than you can see.*

Before I Was a Savage

He knew there would be problems, since this was the beginning, *frontier*. But "it smelled like the end of something." Those were her words, once, before she was carried off. And she was right, right and she knew it—proved it over and over. She stomped a lot of foot and tossed a lot of hair, smugged up her face like a cat with a mouthful of feathers and accused: dead horse there, bloated dog here, rattler in the trough. Misery comforts misery, he said, and it expanded mostly in dust storms, the way the laudanum ran out before the next trip to town. She missed the circus and new beginnings every two days—the way he pitched danger, set her into memory. She died differently then. And yet, every time her foot planted—a new carcass, turkey vulture, worms in the meal—the questions were evident: "What makes us so stitched together?" "Why do my reasons pour out?" The answers, he kept telling her, must be yet.

Little Red Riding Hood Hides Out

She arrives being brave—*I'm being*
very brave—so much of the evidence
has been burned. She arrives trying
harder, having been balled up
at the base of the bed, lying beyond
easily. She's lost the ability to fly
herself through, surrounded
by physicians—or just one of them
with one great light strapped
to his head: "My dear, it seems
that to say 'I' is an admission
you don't want to make."

The Wicked Flee Where No Man Pursueth

I.

She couldn't quite follow how water
was no longer an option, how everything
here hurt when she fell against it. How
she fell. How the husband, the prophet, so
sure with God, had abandoned her
blind as faith would have it.

But they were better afternoons afterward,
swallowing the winking sun—profane,
shameless. Afternoons for memories
of earlier youth: those new concerns
like hunger—she could hear the stars in them.

2.

For marriage, they drew fingers
across their throats, a "cross-my-heart...,"
a "...hope-to-die" ritual. Pulled
through the veil, she felt like a trespass, wed
to distraction: her secret name, her tiny mouth
situation. He said she must shrive. The entire world
pressed between panes of glass.

She would not say that was when
she saw God, but now the prophet had run
off and the fences were falling, needed
mending. What of forgiveness she cannot tell,
but it's coming up on yes.

Little Red Riding Hood through the Eye

At fourteen, her freckles began to open
nightly, shined like tiny miners' caps.
After that, she said, *pleasantly ruined.*
Not what he had said, not "spoiled" as in
"wrecked," not "   ."
Inside her, the fetal bones thrummed
when she found the arrow in the coyote
skull, took it home, grit-in-her-teeth,
flint-scratched. The day after
she paused with her short glass of milk,
felt the edge like a shard: *This is a God test.*
So much it's like rocks in my mouth.
Then his flat palms, his cower, the arrow-twang.

Of Justice Which Punishes, of Mercy Which Pardons (Playing the Chicken Little Card)

He could juggle a spade up his sleeve in a flash, then out—flick—from a lady's ear. Not near exciting as a rubber man, yet everyone said he was more than just top hat and rabbit. Now and again, someone would return from the show and wake up next day *I can see; I can walk; I can hear; My heart beats steady.* And word got around, preceded him town to town: he cured weeping, boils, cold sweats, the cramp, the sob, the broken and old. Some women got the eagers, wanted to hug his neck or snatch a pant leg and force his hands to their foreheads. *This will be good,* we said when they got to our town—that circus: the healer, his wife—*pull up a porch chair, something's afoul.* This quack invades our town, we watch him like a theater show. The children followed, set him up, stole his hat, loosed his horse, took the wife. Evil thing, sure, but those two pulled up their britches like they belonged here—him swirling with rumors of prophecy, holding light in his hands. So they took her, walked her off barefoot in the mountains, crushed her leg with rocks to weight her down. Because he shouldn't have had her—no more than a baby, like she was a bride fell off a wagon; he must have flirted her from her poppa's front porch, whistled Dixie outside their church, hat in hand. Just like him to do some lecherous thing. We were sure that's how they came to be—him and the silent child he sermonized—doubly sure. And we got to bristling. *Not another word,* we warned. But he never searched to find her; he stayed in town, paced like a dog, muttered. He let the show move on, spoke idiot to any visitor who passed, asked if they'd seen her, asked if she'd slid through that slot in the sky, outfoxed the light. Slowly, his dipsomania became legend—something circular and kinetic. He twirled: *This is my body; therefore, I am;* he buried his fingers in the sand, hot glass tinkling along his path. *Glum gun, lily livered, false prophet,* we snarked, our eyes brief weepy spiders, and we left her bleached bones in the hills.

FOUR

Story

Born on a tight sky. Born on a whip snap. His father's shine, his mother's new. Or both. Both like a toy fire engine, a birthday bike. Cake and numbers spun to red. Red gold and crack. Begin again.

Born on a blue return. Born on blue fits. Born because he tied a want. He, his father. He tied a want to knot. His face a stab, a sharp crack. Slime skin, his eye rumpled. Its slow fuzz and snake and snake. Its plucky vein. Rumpled like a quick green tree of knowledge, cheek like a round ripe silk. His name a blanket, a childhood's skin, a new smother. His mother's mark. His father's dime. His snap and fizz. Begin again.

Born the edge of an ax handle. The woodcutter's smooth and round. He became himself: a story, or the beginning of the middle. Because she didn't die. Because the quick bite was a long smile a smile like sleep, the sleep of face. Begin again.

Born on a bread crumb, on a spinning wheel. Born like an eye breaking. An eye breaking into the world. The world breaking into straw.

Everybody Has a Dead Story

It was as if he were watching his own stomach lurch across the river.

Frayed muslin. Chinks in the logs.

Used to live in front of the pain, in front of hurts like his mouth /
tooth misery.

Now this family's in drought.

Said bury *like* burry.

On his knees and face in every creek they come to. Never enough.

Thirsty again.

A grass-plotted dooryard.

At times what he sees is mirage:

Now an empty homestead, an empty horse and corral.

Basin by the bed.

"The oldest girl." "The smart one."

Sourdough. Meat & flies.

Dark, dark, thunder-dark.

Hand in a pan of stew and hair in her face.

Nothing there.

Stalled breath.

Axe.

"Was she there?"

Nothing.

"Cut through a wink & a warning, just like she said."

Crush sounds. Wet sounds.

Cabin fever, they call it.

"She was good at that—that 'don't you use your anger when you talk to me.'"

Hold still.

He thinks of the ways her hand could find his shoulder.

"Where does such thirst come from?"

Smashed jar of pickled eggs. Shards in the sole of her foot.

"Idle hands."

Another little bit for her button box.

The cows are becoming nothing more than ribs.

His head is beating.

They cancel when they collide.

"She's good at making it worse."

Her again, and the children.

A Sunday picnic.

Smoldering wool.

"The boy." "Son."

"He's in heaven, dancing in his glorified body."

They were kneeling like penitents.

They're lined up in the sun; all that is loose
on them flails to the left in the wind.

One said "I shall run"; another "I will fight and die fighting";
and still another, "I will take a gun or a club or...."

Outside, by the well. Lined up.

There never were any children, of course. Sometimes no *her*, either.

"The oldest." "The red-headed one."

A stair-step row of heads.

"Always so quiet, like memory."

Family portrait.

Family Bible.

One made a leg-bail for safety.

Smudged dungarees. Caked.

He goes through every room, rebuking in the name of the Lord.

Hold still.

If he holds his head—just this way—the sweat won't roll into his eyes.

Itinerant Prophet, Soul Paregoric

She measures their tithes
of acorns, haystacks,
potatoes. Stockpiles
of eyelashes, hand-drawn
maps on oilcloth, cotton
batting.

They give her their only
smiles, their forbearance,
their softened pride.
Just the things they can
afford to leave. Barter
for elixirs.

They believe themselves
more than prayer,
ruined with differential
decay, watching her hand snap
open like a wing, a boned
fan to their foreheads.

Her womb is a hive,
the bees make little eating
sounds inside of her.
Her eyes narrow
to elegant spite.

She blesses the congregation
to deliver themselves
before this healing.
Under her hands
their heads are hot
pot roasts, they have
the sun's stink on them.

They feel invisible birds
on their skin, their hearts
shake like wet dogs.
Their tongues spill.
They are hurtling insensible.

This healing makes gravity,
why their bodies fold
back to the dirt
at her deft touch. But gravity,
she knows, is only faith
masquerading, casting laterally.

Shuffle

The magician had gone through ten rabbits unaware—they all pulled the same, he said; they pulled long and not long, they whirled and made dizzy. Backstage, props sobbed and blotted their own slick petals, peeling paint, sticky eyes. *How groggy this light*, he said, *How the sun also stutters.* Backstage, the tiger and the sequin-girls stood guard; the others—saws, scarves, doves—rusted and crumbled in attempts to run off. So, the curtain came down; so, the lights went up. We turned—we always turn—but the room is a box stuck with swords, and he is a pile of silks and handcuffs. He is also running off—the echo of *is this your card* now a language of palm and coin, now the weight of the ace up our sleeve.

Story

Before the paint had dried, his pocket of need
opened a little more. Love fluttered out of the split
like moths. Until then he had thought *paint over it.*
But things grow without warning, and from the absence
leaves were pushing like questions. *How do you retrieve
a lost soul?* So he had to spread out on top, hugging them
down. When the tree fell, it turned model sized,
moss & balsa, and the blood pulled in his feet like roots,
smooth & bright, stretching away from the sun.

Our Hero. His Farce.

Over time, he turned a right pretty piece of calico—the whole town agreed—though we weren't sure what to call it. At the start, it was fingers—slender like twigs. Then two neat thumbs and velvet-smooth palms when he offered his hands: pale apologies. Before this, he had hidden his bodily quarrel—what we named ungodly, what he called *divine*. Before this, he had mocked all womanish things, before his own shapely legs and breasts like ripe plums. So we mocked and jabbed; so we puckered and storied. We had dresses made special, built a booth and sold tickets—*Our town on the map! Our own bearded lady!* But he was soft with thick neck, soft and too broad; he laughed like a thunder, had needs like a beast. So he spit from his mouth this soap-flavored life, left maggoty blunders behind in the sand. So he walked contradiction, in a direction from town.

Put Your Back into It

Like other pilgrims,
lost on his own pass,
the scene of his face
tightened: the reins,
the pull—

This is all I have to give,
he said, and held out his hands
in the gesture that goes with
those words.

To the left, the river
was oil-slick slow.
He couldn't remember
nouns, said *touch-hungry,*
thick-bristle. Gone.

To the left, no way to get
from here to there
without *horse, bridge,*
without one single
handful of God.

The Disappearing Cowboy Trick

He'd felt it at birth—this wreck—he'd
predicted: our days stopping up
that slot in the sky. He'd felt it—that omen,
sun-beaten, that vision. His curse to bear witness,
to proselytize: *They have a stink, these
bodies,* full of nothings and nevers. They're forged
out of woodsharps—our hands full, our eyes.
Less than dolls, he told us. *Your hearts dull
dollars—dented dollars—poor flies.* Thus, this ending,
this moment, this way to unfold; thus, it's done:
quick as thought, our chalk teeth dissolve. Not one
spreads his wings, not one self expunged. Can't
cogitate *scapegrace,* retelling or rapture—
mercy by now a million thumbs in our eyes.

Nobody Hits Me Twice

This house is all hinge, pull, utensil tray:

we use mirrors like dentists—

don't trust our shaking

or the blind corners we have to take.

Use Your Inside Voice

I came at it backward,

which is to say different
from most. A little

more *plunge*; a little less

buck. Hat held high, in
one hand; ropes gripped

tight, the other. That *was*,
as I said, before. Now, face

pushed forward, through
the surface. Face pushed
outward, into a tangle.

Our Hero, His Quote Unquote

He wasn't a bootlicker, that's for sure—that spine-straight, razor-spurred, look-you-in-the-eye kind of guy was only a bit staled—the town had just moved on without him. We agreed he'd never catch up, so we indulged, acted all accounts like she was the present tense he used: *You're right. Her eyes are hoofed and shadowed. Sure, she's something duplicitous—a twitchy liar.* He'd nod, satisfied, walk on, return. Fact is, no one's sure where she's gone—out at the first whistle-stop, or he ended her before she ever could've left. Can't blame it, either way—she was always a bit dismal and drab—her mouth closed like a lid, her face an abuse. A very unique thing, that conflict of souls. All you need for that madness is one idea of plot, one infinitesimal paranoia. And all we do in town—all we've ever done—is take bitter measure of the arithmetic of that path.

I Thought This Was Supposed to Be a Shoot-'Em-Up

I.

Pretend was over—just like that. Because he got so caught up in the sky, he forgot you can't catch the horizon in a day, can't cross a mountain without sleeping in some caves. Ever since, his life was smeared with anger.

2.

He arrived with a drink in his hand, a gun in his holster. Cocksure and mouthing undesirables, blowing his skank breath. He didn't have to shoot, just disrupted the air—his very own turbulence, a change in pressure all around us.

3.

We had a conundrum: how do you stop an exploding man? (*Explosion* as in *storm*, *storm* as in *weather*.) You'd better have some bricks in your britches, some sand in your craw; no falling in love with falling in love. (Bull-by-the-horns stuff.)

4.

We learned to let him be, as we left the buzzards to pick out eyes, unsure how one thing causes another. We knew enough to know that all men hurt, they hurt and are inconsolable offenders afterward.

Dig

One choice is to

not talk, I say,

wonder what that

admits. Another

is to participate

in the myth-

making. Move

like tiny creatures

at the bottom of

the sea. After

which, freeze-

dried, rasping,

stuck all over

with pins.

Our Hero Has Run

We can see her life through the shutter slats, face parsed out in billets of time: years of mouth gash, years of wretch, years of histrionic gasp. Years tangled and wind-frayed, her head like a thistle; her static & panic; her *run to the house, drift with the flood*; her *flee*. And now she's a mess of salt cod & cure, fixed like Lot's wife, hung from these beams. This is her wreck; we're altered and tear-chapped— *our work of plunder; our work post-slaughter.* The effect: her echo—a trifling galaxy, a fragile idea of the first place he left her, fashioning dress patterns, fashioning dinner. Here, we forsake her—here, in the barn making left-handed Saturns.

Notes

"Insidious Dream Waltz": Title from a line in a song by Andrew Bird.

JornatadelMuerto is Spanish for "journey of the dead"; the Jornada del Muerto is also the name of a dangerous pioneer trail in the Southwest.

"The Wicked Flee Where No Man Pursueth": *Proverbs 28:1*.

"Born like an eye breaking": inspired by Robert Creeley.

"I shall run"; "I will fight and die fighting"; "I will take a gun or a club or...." quoted in Captivity Of The Oatman Girls: Being An Interesting Narrative Of Life Among The Apache And Mohave Indians, In 1851; The Narrow Escape Of Lorenzo D. Oatman; The Capture of Olive A. And Mary A. Oatman As Given By Lorenzo D. And Olive A. Oatman by Royal B. Stratton.

Many lines and phrases inspired by language in *Cowboy Lingo* by Ramon F. Adams.

Acknowledgments

Thanks to the following publications, in which many of the poems in this manuscript first appeared:

5th Gear; Abridged; American Letters & Commentary; Anti-; Best New Poets, 2005; Big Bridge; Buffalo Carp; California Quarterly; CAB/ NET; Coconut; Conceit Magazine; The Concher; Court Green; CRATE; Gertrude; Handful of Dust; High Plains Register; Horse Less Review; Iodine Poetry Journal; Letterbox; LIT; OVS Magazine; Pacific Review; Parcel; Poetry Pacific; Psychic Meatloaf; Queen City Review; Quiddity; Rattle; Redactions: Poetry, Poetics, & Prose; The Reprint; Skidrow Penthouse; Switchback; Texas Poetry Calendar; Tusculum Review; Weave Magazine; Western Press Books 2012 Anthology.

Some poems in this manuscript have also appeared in Little Red Riding Hood Missed the Bus, a chapbook (Subito Press, 2005).

Special Thanks

Special thanks to the UCROSS Foundation, whose generous residency made possible much of the work in this manuscript.

Additional thanks to Dawn Dawson Wexo, proprietor of the Occidental Hotel in Buffalo, Wyoming, who kindly allowed me the use of her historic rooms for immersion, writing and inspiration.

Kristin Abraham

Kristin Abraham was born and raised in Michigan. She currently lives in Fort Collins, Colorado, with her husband, three dogs and two cats. She teaches English at a community college in Wyoming and serves as editor-in-chief and poetry editor for the literary journal *Spittoon* (www.spittoonmag.com).